Pregnancy

Why didn't anyone warn me about some of this shit?

by Jennie Breeden

www.TheDevilsPanties.com

A semi autobiographical webcomic about life, the universe, and everything. This is a compilation of the comics about pregnancy.
Spoilers, everything turns out fine.

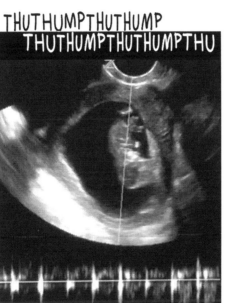

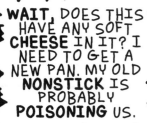

PREGNANCY FACT # 382

NO MATTER HOW MANY TIMES YOU GO TO THE BATHROOM...

... AS SOON AS YOU LEAVE THE HOUSE, YOU WILL HAVE TO PEE.

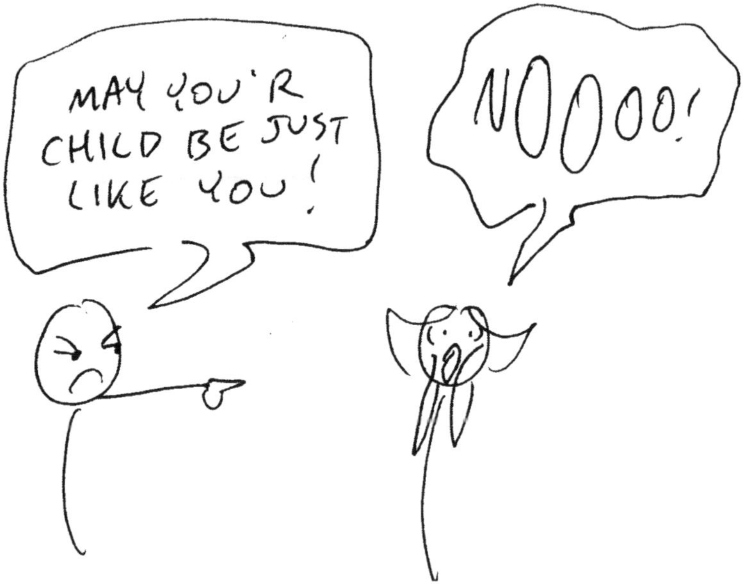
MAY YOU'R CHILD BE JUST LIKE YOU!
NOOOO!

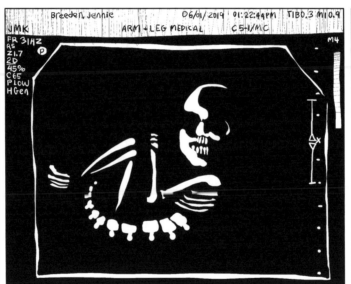

FIRST MONTH PREGNANCY

SIXTH MONTH PREGNANCY

20170916BABY
OKAY, WAIT, I KNOW SHE KICKS ME IN THE SIDE...
...BUT THEN THERE'S THIS LUMP AT MY RIBS, HER BUTT?
AND HICCUPS ARE BETWEEN MY HIPS... SO...
? ?

I **JUST** REALIZED THAT BABIES EVENTUALLY TURN INTO **PRETEENS**...

... CAN WE START SAVING UP FOR SLEEP AWAY CAMP?

WE'VE ACTUALLY GOT A COUPLES **COSTUME** FOR DRAGON CON **RAMBLING** THIS YEAR!

NEAT! IT'S NOT SOME CLICHÉ **PREGNANT** COSTUME, IS IT?

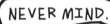

NEVER MIND.

GOD **DAMN** IT SHREDDER!

SHE'S BUTT **FIRST**, SO WE HAVE TO GET HER TURNED **AROUND**. TRY HANDSTANDS IN A **POOL**, CAT/COW **YOGA**, COLD AND WARM **COMPRESS**, AND WE'LL SCHEDULE YOU FOR A **MANUAL** SPIN, BUT WE LIKE HER TO DO IT ON HER **OWN**...

... HERE'S THE NUMBER FOR A GOOD **ACUPUNCTURIST**.

OH **NO**, I DON'T LIKE **NEEDLES**.

IF WE CAN'T GET HER HEAD **DOWN** THEN WE'LL HAVE TO DO A **C-SECTION**.

OKAY! **SO!** HANDSTANDS, YOGA, ICE PACK, AND WHAT WAS THAT **NEEDLE** NUMBER AGAIN??

THIS HOSPITAL IS **CLOSER** BUT DOESN'T HAVE A HIGH **RISK** AREA IF WE'D NEED IT. LET'S TAKE A TOUR AND SEE WHAT WE THINK.

WE HAVE A **PREP** ROOM, THEN THE **BIRTHING** ROOM, AND A **RECOVERY** ROOM WITH PULL OUT **BED** FOR DAD WHERE YOU STAY THE **NIGHT** AND HAVE A **FANCY** BREAKFAST WITH SPARKLING **APPLE** JUICE IN **CHAMPAIGNE** GLASSES.

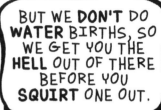

THIS FACILITY HAS A **JACUZZI** ROOM TO HELP A LABORING MOM **RELAX**.

BUT WE **DON'T** DO **WATER** BIRTHS, SO WE GET YOU THE **HELL** OUT OF THERE BEFORE YOU **SQUIRT** ONE OUT.

OKAY, I GOT OUR HOSPITAL **GO** BAG PUT TOGETHER.

RAQUET BALLS FOR MASSAGE AND **STRESS** SQUEEZING, MUSIC, **PHONE** CHARGERS, **EAR** BUDS, MINTS, **LIP** BALM, ROBE, **SLIPPERS**, THREE CHANGES OF **CLOTHES**, TOILETRIES, SWIMSUIT, **GAMES**, BLANKET, PILLOW, RELAXATION **FOCUS** ITEM, SNACKS, NOTES, **SKETCHBOOK**, GAMEBOY.

HOW MANY DAYS DO YOU EXPECT TO **STAY** IN THE HOSPITAL?

ABOUT TWO.

BONUS!

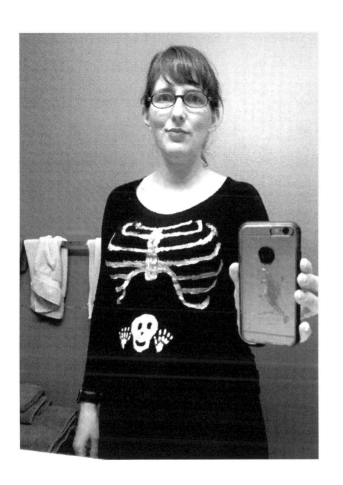
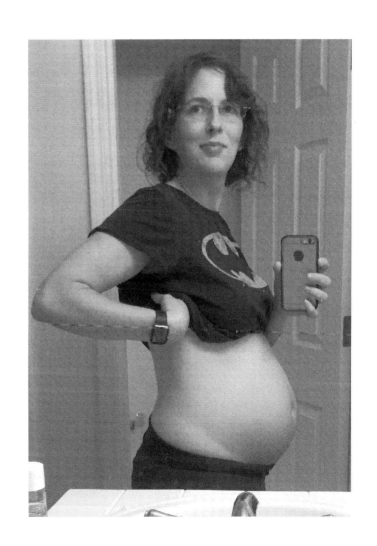

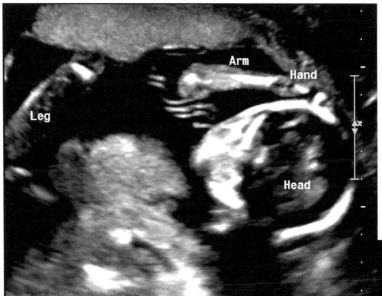

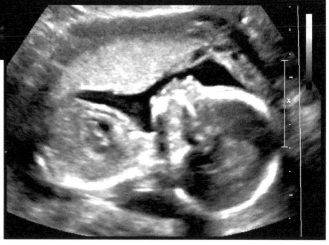

THEDEVILSPANTIES.COM

Made in the USA
Columbia, SC
15 August 2024

40563074R00089